T0366056

STEVEN CHARLES KANUMBA

The Great Fallen Tree.

Emmanuel Zirimwabagabo

AuthorHouse™
1663 Liberty Drive
Bloomington, IN 47403
www.authorhouse.com
Phone: 1-800-839-8640

Published by AuthorHouse: 12/05/2014

ISBN: 978-1-4969-5217-2 (sc)
ISBN: 978-1-4969-5218-9 (e)

This book is printed on acid-free paper.

1984-2012

To die in love for someone is not the big thing, but to live with that pain with a smile forever is the real great achievement.

Contents

INTRODUCTION. 1

EARLY LIFE OF STEVEN CHARLES KANUMBA 3

FLORA MUTEGOA. 7

STEVEN KANUMBA'S RELATIONSHIPS 9

STEVEN KANUMBA'S CAREER 13

STEVEN KANUMBA AND OTHER PROJECTS IN THE COMMUNITY 59

STEVEN KANUMBA'S DEATH 61

DIRECTING A MOVIE 65

APPRECIATION PAGE 81

The Great Fallen Tree.

Love is what makes men co-exist. It does not matter what you are, who you are or where you have been, but by the end of the day all of us will be judged.**-Episcopere Emmanuel**

Steven Kanumba's memories will never fade in many, especially both in Tanzania and in all his fans across the world. He was an actor, a singer, a writer, a director, a producer, a comedian and a mentor to many.

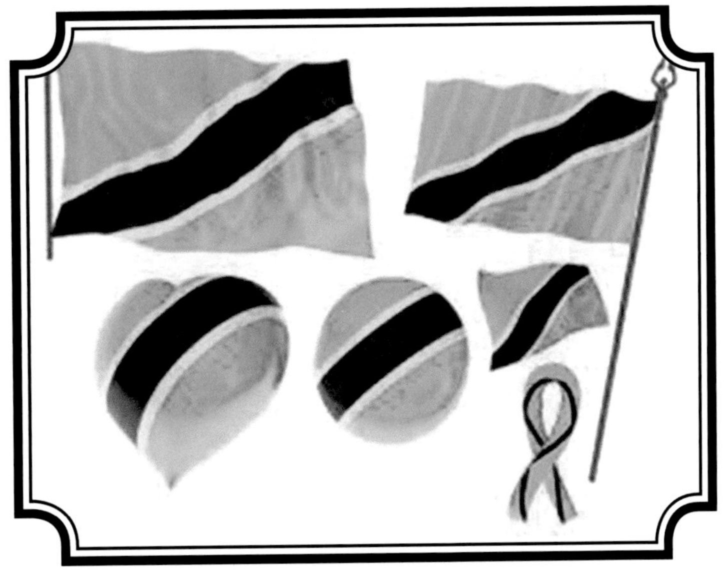

STEVEN CHARLES KANUMBA

All content and names used in this book have exclusively been authorized by the relevant authorities. Any form of information written in this book has been given out in good confidence and for the purpose of learning and not to discriminate anyone who worked or interacted with the late Steven Kanumba.

INTRODUCTION.

Steven Charles Kanumba was born in Ngokolo in Shinyanga, Tanzania on 8th of January, 1984. He was the last born son and only son of Charles Kusekwa Meshack Kanumba and Flora Mutegoa. He had two older sisters, Vedastina Mshumbusi and Abela Kajumulo. He studied in Bugoyi primary school and later did his secondary studies at Mwadui Secondary School. It was not easy for him during his early years of education as he encountered school fees problems. This was because he had been brought up by his mother who was not financially stable by then. In Form 2, he transferred to Vosa Mission Secondary School in Dar es Salaam, where he completed his Form Four Education. He later pursued further education at JKT Jitegemee Secondary School in the city. He received special training with Dr Nyoni at the University of Dar es Salaam, which served as a major stepping stone for his mainstream acting career. Doctor Nyoni personally mentored him and supervised his learning project for three months. By the year 2002 he was already a member of the famous Kaole Sanaa Group, participating in a number of television shows on ITV Station. Before joining Kaole Sanaa Group, Steven had already displayed talent in singing church songs and acting in school and church productions. While at Kaole Sanaa Group, he participated in various shows with ITV which included, Jahazi, Dira, Zizimo, Tufani, Sayari, Taswira, Baragumu and Gharika. This gave him fame and opened him up to the world of film industry. He later left the group in the year 2006, and started his film acting career with a company known as Game First Quality. This was his stepping stone to greater heights as he featured films like 'She is My Sister' 'Dar to Lagos' 'Cross My Sin' 'The Director' 'Hero of the Church'. He also worked with some of the leading Nollywood artistes like Mercy Johnson, Nkiru Silvanus, Femi Ogedegbe and Ramsey Nuoah. He managed to scoop several awards. Among the awards won by Steven Kanumba were, IJUMAA Sexiest male bachelor of the year-2006, Best Actor of the Year (Baab Kubwa Magazine)-2006, the Best Actor in Tanzania (Hollywood John Wayne International Awards)-2007, Honorary Award (Tanzania Film Vinara Awards)-2008, Best Actor-2007-2008 (SHIVIWATA) and best actor, best director -Film Central-2010 among others. Before the age of thirty years, he had achieved so much, yet his film industry had just begun. He looked forward for long and a fruitful career in every area of this industry. His name had become a household name as he was a multi award winning actor, with a career spanning almost a decade. He had also become a very active philanthropist. This was due to the many books he had read in order to understand humanity. He had grown to be a man of the people too. He was involved in many charitable activities. Due to this he had been appointed as the OXFAM GROW ambassador for Tanzania. He was also actively involved in the activities of ZANTEL, STAR TIME and JOHN WYNE. He had grown to be appreciated in every step of his career by everyone who knew him. Success was his story.

EARLY LIFE OF STEVEN CHARLES KANUMBA

His father, Charles Kanumba and his mother, Flora Mutegoa brought him up to be what he was. Every step of his life had significance mark towards his destiny.

Growing up from a very humble background and rising up to be a star was a spectacular thing. He was a bright and energetic boy. His mother was focused to bring up a boy who was going to leave a mark to the world. She was determined to go through all by herself. As an African woman she worked hard to bring up all her children. She was did all chores that could give her money to facilitate that. She worked hard to make sure her son and all other children grew up well, though it was not easy for her.

It was not long before Kanumba grew up to being a strong, energetic, a very determined, intelligent and a focused boy. From his early age he had always wanted to live with his father who lived in another town. This was not easy as his father lived far away in Dar es Salaam and he lived miles away in the village with his mother. His mother was hesitant to let go of her son, but finally did so. Steven believed since he was a man he had a lot to learn from his father. It was not by choice too, life had developed a lot of difficulties as his mother could no longer raise his school fees. It was a joyous time to meet his larger family in Dar es Salaam. His mother had no problem with that as all she wanted was a bright future for her son. His father embraced him and welcomed him. He was well received and he adjusted very fast as he had grown up in the village. His mother was far away and he had to learn more from his father.

Steven started going to school and made many friends in the city too. His new life with his new family not only opened him up to new opportunities but also to new challenges. He also kept on going back to Shinyanga to check often on his mother, who was his best friend too.

Steven Kanumba's Family

Being a young man full of dreams, he encountered several challenges that made him grow wiser and focused in life. In his early ages of life he lived with his grandmother, Shuzana. They lived together with many other relatives. The house was always full and he had learned to live with everyone too. He never got a chance of having a private life. It was through his early life that he acquired the spirit of team work and love.

Living with his mother in one town and his father in another town was challenging. He had to work hard as the culture demanded. Being the only boy child in his family, he had to prove his sense of responsibility to everyone. He worked diligently at home and in school. This made everyone in his family look up to him all the time. He would wake up very early in the morning to make breakfast for everyone. He would sleep very late after everyone had gone to sleep. At the age of twelve years, he was very responsible. He knew that he needed to be strong as he had very big dreams. The older he grew the more responsibilities added up to his life.

He made sure that he spent equal time with his both parents though they lived in different towns. He simply had the best mother in the entire world. His father too had taught him all the cultures and what was expected of him as he grew up. He knew that he was lucky to have his parents on his side all the time. He also got the love of his two older sisters. Everyone simply loved him very much.

They encouraged him all the time and were always proud of him. He was determined to excel in life. All he needed was to finish school first. He knew something was going to spring up out of his life someday. He spent his free time in church singing and acting plays. He had joined his church choir at AIC Kambarage in Shinyanga and AIC Chang'ombe in Dar es Salaam. It was through this, that he discovered his talents. He enjoyed every opportunity to sing in public or do any presentation without fear. He would always remember his mother's words of affirmation. She kept on saying that it did not matter what life brought up, God was always in control of everything. He trusted God more than anyone else in his life.

He became an encourager of his friends who were going through frustrations. To him, he had become immune to challenges. In fact, they were his stepping stones. He started to become a star and used every opportunity he got to do all he could. He knew too well his talents were his destiny. His mother became a point of reference. She was his mentor, a friend and his blessing. He made sure he did everything his mother and his father wanted him to do without complaining. Through his obedience, he learnt how to live well with the outside world. Nothing was a challenge to him. He knew that it was only through education that he was going to shine in life. He was not ready to give up for his dreams. When he felt like giving up, he would spare time and go back to Shinyanga to spend moments with his mother. His mother seemed to understand him more than anybody else in the whole world. She gave him the true meaning of life. She was there to encourage him all the time. He had all reasons to excel in life. He believed strongly that every good thing in life came through sacrifice.

Good character was also part of success in his life.

FLORA MUTEGOA.

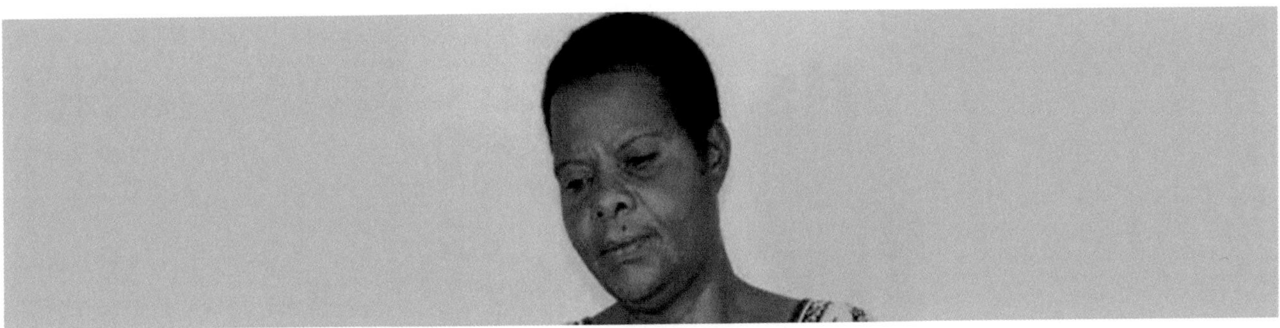

Flora Mutegoa was more than an ordinary woman. She rose above the proverbial woman. She was full of strength and honor, and she was ready to bring up her children in the best way, with no fear. She worked against all odds to make sure her son succeeded in all spheres of life.

Though she lived in a different town from her husband, she was determined to bring her children in the best way. She worked hard every day of her life as was expected of her. Living together with her mother was easier for her too. She watched her son grow up gracefully. She made sure her son never missed any opportunity to get what he needed at any time.

She had trained his son to do all manner of household chores. He was good at working in the farm and even looking after goats. She had also brought him up in a godly way by taking him to church since he was young. Kanumba was talented in public speaking. He was always appointed as a leader since he was young boy. He was a leader in both school and in church. He had learned how to speak Sukuma, Swahili and English languages.

His mother knew his son was very talented. She never missed an opportunity to give him the chance to join any group he wanted to join from his early age. She encouraged him to join clubs in school and participate fully in church choir. She also encouraged him to read widely. This made Steven to develop the love of reading.

At one point, Steven composed a song and dedicated it to her.

These were the words of the song, See them on the road, the babies are on their back, our mothers they go the market and get all the need for the household! Today we don't think of them, we even disrespect them! Let's respect and give them praises, let's get advices from them mama Africa! Thank you mother for your goodness and all that you have done for me! In you mother I stayed in your womb for nine months and every time you bore all my shame when I did anything wrong! I thank you mother Kanumba, my Flora, my mother. You went hungry so that I can go to school. You borrowed money so that I can have a meal I say thank you, even when you grow old, I will value you. It is praise to treasure our mothers.

STEVEN KANUMBA'S RELATIONSHIPS

Kanumba's first relationship started with one of Shinyanga girl, where he grew up in his early life. Kanumba loved this girl very much but she never reciprocated back.

Steven Kanumba was handsome, young and classy. He was a go-getter. He had met this girl in Mwadui secondary school. He liked her company but the girl was not happy with him as he had no money. He gave her all hopes for future but she was never interested in him. He had not thrived in the acting industry. He was still a student. When he completed his secondary school studies, he continued to send letters and cards to her but she did not respond. This made him to quit the relationship though he was hurt. Not until he started appearing on Tanzania screens, the girl came back to ask him to continue with the relationship. She knew now he was a celebrity and had the money too. He however turned down the girl and moved on. He saw her as an opportunist.

His fame had hit every media house in East Africa. He was now a celebrity and had to make right choices in his relationship life.

He had another relationship with a beauty contestant who had won Miss Tanzania 2006, Wema Sepetu. She represented Tanzania in Miss World contest 2006 which was held in Poland.

Their meeting with Steven was coincidental rather than pre-planned. She had gone for shopping in a furniture mall in Dar es Salaam with her sister who she was staying with. She had chosen to stay with her sister instead of her mother in order to have freedom with her friends. At the furniture mall, however there seemed to be an event there. A shooting session was going on. Everyone seemed not to be shopping, but had given way to the actors. Just like other shoppers, they had no choice but to stare too. Wema Sepetu was a very beautiful lady that anyone could not take his or eyes off her. She was not so much interested either but just not cause attention too she kept close to her sister. This movie cast had a scene at the furniture mall and had generated a lot interest to the public. All over sudden, she noticed Steven Kanumba. They had eye to eye contact. They could not stop from staring at each other. By then, Steven Kanumba was shooting a film called Lost Twins. The whole area was actually flooded with other Tanzanian actors. At that point Steven walked straight on and greeted her. He asked her a chance to talk to her after the session, of which she agreed. After the session, they met. Steven poured a lot of praises on her beauty. Although she was a celebrity, she still was reserved for the sake of her reputation too. Steven Kanumba begged her to join the acting industry but she said that she needed to consult with her parents first. Steven felt happy and privileged to have met her. They exchanged telephone numbers. They were all excited to meet each other. She had seen him severally on screens and now they had even met face to face. Steven was already looking forward to work with her in his movies as she was stunningly beautiful. She did not resist any other invite to meet him another day as she already liked him even from the movies. They parted after many minutes of familiarization. They were both extremely excited and looking forward for another meeting. Steven made sure he called her the same day just to be sure that she had saved his number on her phone. They talked severally after that and they were seen several places together. Their affair was no longer a secret to the world. Steven was up again in love with the beauty queen. On the other side, she still was a bit reserved. They would eat together, walk together and enjoy life together, sooner than later she accepted and affirmed their affair. Steven was very fast to introduce her to the acting world. He persuaded her to join him and act a movie together. It was not as easy for her as she felt that it was not her talent to do that. Steven introduced her to his boss in Mtitu Game and she soon became accustomed. She was consistently coached and directed. They acted together the movie, "point of no return" They would meet every day for rehearsals. This strengthened their love for each other. They finally shot the movie. She found it easier than she expected. Everybody liked her ability to learn fast too. Unfortunately she had to fly to Malaysia for her further studies in Business Management. This separated her from her lover. Since they were both young, they knew soon they will meet again. She later received a copy of the movie she had acted out while in Malaysia. That is when she realized that she had a talent in the film industry too, after watching herself in the same movie. Her friends too encouraged her to pursue that world of theatre, as they realized that she had a talent. Years flew very fast and she was back in Tanzania after her studies. She then decided to give more of her time to the film industry. During this time, their relationship with Steven Kanumba was also strengthened. They acted together more movies. Among them were Red Valentine, Family Tears, White Maria and many more. It was through him that she re-discovered her talent.

Their relationship thrived on well, till they had a disagreement. This brewed a lot of trouble in her relationship with Steven Kanumba. They no longer enjoyed a peaceful friendship. They finally parted ways but still remained friends. Since they were in the same career, they learned to live with their differences.

It was after this relationship, Steven started dating Nargis Mohamed. Their relationship had a religion barrier as she was a Muslim.

Steven made her picture the cover picture of the movie called Magic House. They loved each other but their religion background restrained them.

This did not go for long so they had to break up. Steven started another affair with Sylvia Shali, who had won the beauty pageant as Miss Kinondoni. Life with her was wonderful. They even lived together as a man and wife. They soon began to have a lot of disagreements too. Their love life was frequently featured by the media.

One day, Steven travelled to America to shoot one of his movies. While he was away, the media kept on following their private lives. By the time he came back to Tanzania, news about them was everywhere.

Their relationship broke up as he loved private life. He started another affair with Aunt Ezekiel. No one could understand about their relationship as it was very secretive.

They too broke up, and he started dating an 18-year old girl, Elizabeth Michael, her cast name was Lulu. That was early 2012. However it was very secretive. The media had nothing to say about their love life till the day Steven Kanumba died. She later confessed that they were both lovers as she was with him in his bedroom the night he passed away. Lulu became a talk of the whole world as she faced charges concerning Steven Kanumba.

STEVEN KANUMBA'S CAREER

At the age of six years, Steven Kanumba joined his church choir. This was the influx of his gift in life. He sang passionately and this singled him out as a young God-fearing man. His talent was outstanding to everyone who saw him at that tender age. He was never interested in singing secular music. He knew very well there were no morals in the secular world. At the age of 18 years, he tried to join the Kaole Sanaa Group. His application was rejected as the managers thought he was very young and inexperienced. Most of the actors and actresses in this group had been fully trained He did everything to convince them but in vain. He however did not give up. He would attend all their shows and still kept on applying.

But one day, an elderly lady named Madam Mwenda pleaded with the management of the group and he was finally approved of joining. She had watched the passion and the zeal in him and the many tireless journeys he had made to join the team, and saw and extra ordinary talent.

This is how he got his chance to explore his talent. This lady had believed in him and would give him a lot of motherly advice and tips of success in the same industry. After joining this group, he encountered more challenges than expected. He had to lie to his mother to get more money for transport, as he had to go after school extra hours. Kaole Sanaa Group staged their plays in a place known as Magomeni "Lango la Jiji" in Dar es Salaam. This was far away from his school. The challenge of time and distance was not a barrier at all to him. One day, during the rehearsals at the group, a cell phone of one of the members went missing. When the inspection was done, unfortunately it was found in his bag. This was a very big embarrassment to him. He could not defend himself so it was decided that he was to be expelled from the group. Madam Mwenda defended him and said that he must have been innocent and someone else had put the phone in his bag. This created a lot of commotion as she threatened to visit a Tanzanian witchdoctor to expose the thief. This got worse as it was to be a bad publicity of the group by then. Madam Mwenda was very much convinced that it was not Steven Kanumba who had hidden the cell phone in his bag. She knew it was a mischief from one of the members, who never liked him. One of the members later admitted to have hidden it himself in his bag. This saw everyone trust Steven Kanumba in the entire group. Thanks to Madam Mwenda who had believed in him. Steven had found another mother in his world of acting. He was accepted and loved by everyone from then and it was through this group that he joined fully the theatre world. Through his dedication and commitment, he featured in different television programmes, like Jahazi, Dira and his film debut in Haviliki. These were all soap operas organized from this group.

In the year 2006, Steven Kanumba met Nazz who connected him and introduced him to actors in Lagos. This was successfully carried out by Mtitu Game that featured both Nigerian and Tanzanian actors. It is from this new connection that birthed new films like "She is my sister", "This is it" and "Love gable". These movies that he acted out with Nigerian actors not only brought out his ability to do better but exposed him to the whole world. He was determined to reach the peak of his dream. He was determined to collaborate with other artistes from any part of the world. He knew that he was not born to be a local champion but the best in the world. He grasped every opportunity that came his way and saw it as a stepping stop to greater heights. He was well received by the Nollywood world and they all loved his enthusiasm to venture and discover new talents in the industry. Having been born in Tanzania, his spoken Swahili was better than English. The opportunity to act with the Nollywood actors and actresses gave him the opportunity to improve his English too.

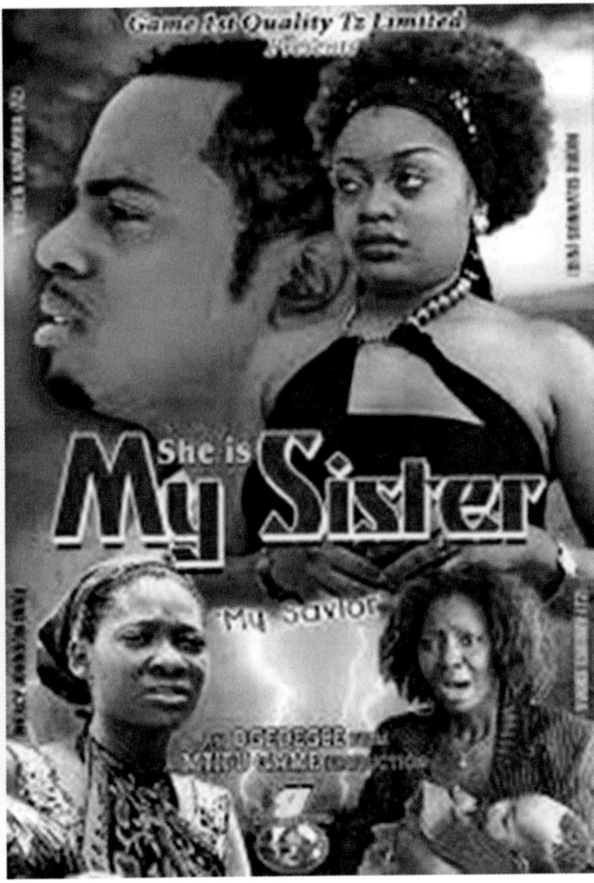

This made him also among the first actor to collaborate with other actors from another country. Everyone wanted to find out who exactly he was. The country Tanzania became too a country of focus, as wherever his name was mentioned, his country was also mentioned.

The movie that featured Mercy Johnson, "She is My Sister", was the talk of the movie fans. It had a very good plot that kept every viewer stirred up. It was also through this that his popularity sprang up in Nigeria. In his tender age he had already started acting with the most popular actors and actresses in Nollywood. He actually became the man to watch for his next steps.

This greatly improved the film industry in Tanzania with many joining the industry as a career.

Back in Tanzania, he was the king of the screens and a favorite to every Tanzanian. His talent as a comedian, actor and writer was evident to everyone

This came with a lot of great sacrifice too. This has been evident from the other actors. They have consistently followed his footsteps and have been ready to learn.

Steven Kanumba remains an icon in Tanzania that will be remembered forever. His name is synonym to the film industry.

Some of the dramas that he acted on national televisions include:

- Jahazi
- Dira
- Zizimo
- Tufani
- Sayari
- Taswira

- Gharika
- Baragumu

He had managed to capture the attention of every Tanzanian and he was a favorite to watch in every home.

One of the media houses in Tanzania had an interview with him about his career life and he had this to say,

"As an actor, you can do what you want with your role. That's why they hire you; to take the role and make it real. Wherever you go, whatever you are doing and whatever is happening around you, always take your own sunshine with you. Keep a hopeful attitude as an act of defiance in the tough times. Don't let the weather control your mood and don't let events control your attitude. If you can change things, do. If you can't, choose who you're going to be."

Steven Kanumba had become an expert. He would take up any role in the play and by the end of it he would carry the day. To him, adjusting to play any role was very simple. Having interacted with the high and mighty in the industry, he had become focused to reach his goal.

Some of the films that Steven Kanumba featured included;

Sikitiko Langu

Sikitiko Langu: A movie that featured in the year 2006. This featured a lady who hurt the church by pretending and camouflaging who she was. She finally reveals her identity and leaves everyone in shock. Was she forgiven or accepted?

Dangerous Desire

Dangerous Desire: Steven Kanumba featured in this movie in the year 2006. This brings a man who goes ahead and marries the sister to the wife, simply because his wife cannot conceive. A battle co-exists between two sisters who begin a battle just for one man. The quest to get married and have a marriage with children births out a dangerous desire. What was the fate of such a couple?

Penina

Penina: Steven Kanumba featured in this movie of Penina in the year 2007. This is a sad movie full of regrets that featured one ambitious lady who gave up on her esteem and marriage, to go for other things in life. When sense dawns on her it is too late either. What happens to her marriage?

Cross My sin

Cross My sin: In 2007, Steven Kanumba tried to play his movies in English instead of Swahili Language. "I seek peace in my heart. I have chosen the right way. I will stand by the truth even if it will cost me my life." The movie featured Mercy Johnston and other Nollywood actors. This was a talk of every household. Having a good background with his church culture, he got the opportunity to cast movies that were church centered, and this was one of it. This movie opened up his world and got the opportunity to cast all fears when acting in English language.

A movie that one cannot afford to watch once but several times!

A point of No return

A point of No return: He acted out this movie in the year 2008. A movie that was widely watched not only Tanzania but in the entire African continent. The movie was acted out in Swahili but was also subtitled for the comfort of any viewer. This was the first movie he acted out with Wema Sepetu, his once girlfriend. It featured a lady that was married off to a rich and devil worshipping family. In quest to prevent the marriage, she gives herself to another man. The fight for evil, her life and even marriage keeps her on toes.

Did she give up on her marriage?

What happened to her lover?

Did evil overcome light?

White Maria

White Maria: This movie featured Wema Sepetu too as a major character. A movie acted on spectacular scenes and environment, a fight between one's dirty past and the present life. The impact of abortion and death of innocent lives haunts a man to a point of surrendering his life to God.

What happens to his marriage?

Did God forgive him?

This movie brought out Steven Kanumba's talent of acting to the whole world.

The lost Twins

The lost Twins: This also one of the movies that got a lot of attention from Tanzania. It features twins that separated when they were young. The hatred towards a mother is so great for concealing such a matter.

Oprah

Oprah: This movie featured on screens for the first time in 2008.It focuses on repaying back good for evil. This has a great lesson for many viewers especially in society. Can secrets destroy relationships?

The Village Pastor

The Village Pastor: This movie also featured in 2008. This movie rotates on a village Pastor who marries an unfaithful wife. She messes up his reputation and he is torn apart with the voice of the church and his consciousness.

Will a pastor divorce his wife because of her unfaithfulness?

Will the wife change to please the church?

The Stolen Will

The Stolen Will: This movie featured in 2009. Will a dead man's wish be followed way after he has died or will what makes sense and greediness take the day?

Red Valentine

Red Valentine: Steven featured in this movie in 2009. A stirring movie that focuses on true love and the battle involved in love.

Who, where and what is Red valentine?

Family Tears

Family Tears: Treating right every family member regardless of their present circumstances. This movie featured Wema Sepetu too in the year 2008.

What is greater, the power of love or the power of a family?

Magic House

Magic House: Steven featured in this movie in the year 2010. Nargis Mohammed, one of his girlfriends became a major cast in the movie.

Why did Steven Kanumba use Nargis Mohammed in this movie?

Was it because of her religion or abilities?

Find out, why the movie was called magic house.

Fake Smile

Fake Smile: A smile does not simply mean the person is happy. It could be a plastic smile or they could be the most depressed person in the society. Everybody needs love.

How does a genuine smile look like?

Unfortunate Love

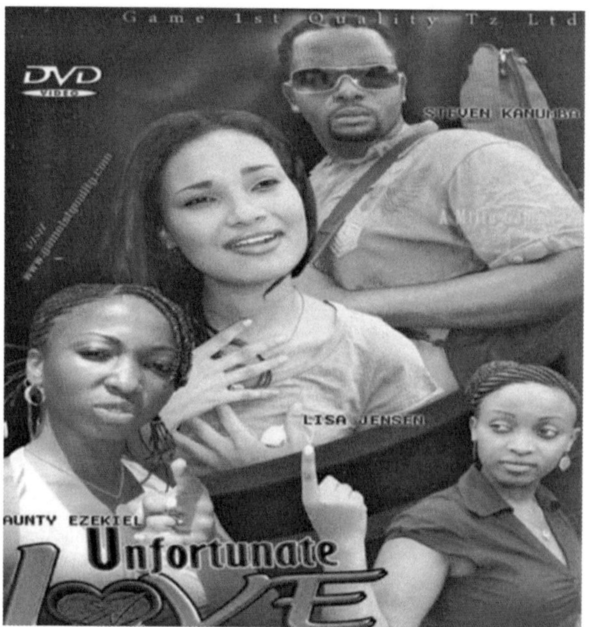

Unfortunate Love: It takes a minute to have a crush on someone, an hour to like someone and a day to love someone but it takes a lifetime to forget someone.

Aunt Ezekiel, one of his girlfriends featured in this particular movie. They had met in the film industry.

What happens when your true love ends up being a disastrous one?

The hero of the Church

The hero of the Church: A movie that demonstrates the reality of religion. He physically fights spiritual faith and wins the battle. Steven Kanumba being a major cast fights the lies those congregations have to put up with and brings out the truth.

How does one fight a pulpit fight? Who will betray the church?

Will he win a battle of sharks?

Will the flock believe in their shepherd or one of the flocks?

Saturday Morning

Saturday Morning: A movie that was acted out with diligence. A man marries and ends up staying with a friend instead of his wife?

What happens when another woman walks in when the pastor is just about to call it a marriage? An intriguing movie full of love, risks and hatred, with great lessons to learn.

Crazy Love

Crazy Love: A movie that he featured as an academic professor. He demonstrates the power of love verses madness. He compares love to a disease that has no cure. Before featuring and directing this movie he read books by Plato, Karl Max, Alexander the great, Samuel Taylor. He needed to discover human behavior in times of love.

Can love cause madness?

More than pain

More than pain: Two teenagers studying at a seminary school fall in love and start messing around, the girl gets pregnant and she gets expelled from school. Soon the boy responsible gets caught and he also gets expelled from school, and they soon start living together.

People fear death even more than pain. It's strange that they fear death. Life hurts a lot more than death. At the point of death, the pain is over. Yeah, I guess it is a friend.

A movie full of tears and full of expectations too.

Young billionaire

Young billionaire: A movie that features a flamboyant life of a rich man verses true love. He falls in love with a prostitute who sleeps with his best man on the wedding day. Will this marriage last?

Uncle JJ

Uncle JJ: A man living in the rural areas with his niece and nephew. He believes that educating a girl is just waste of time and money, so he only takes the boy to school and he leaves the girl at home.

Will the myth of a boy being always the best and the reliable child stand the test of time?

This is it

This is it: A story about an Uncle that tries to raise his late sister's kids (a girl and boy). Living with them has become an issue because of the little girl's behavior.

Will an unknown power that controls the girl lose its grip or will destroy the entire family?

Will a pastor save the disaster that hits this man's family?

Off Side

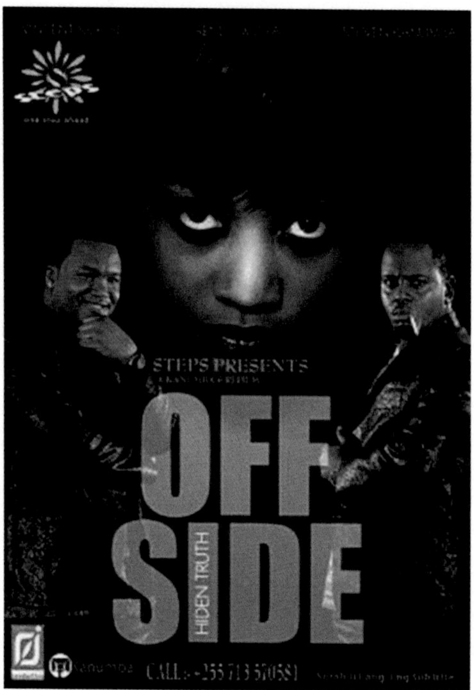

Off Side: A battle of two sons, a father and a step mother.

Find out, who seduces who or who fell in love. A step mother kills the husband so that he can get married to the son. He then plots to sleep with all sons. The lastborn son gets into trap. The elder son remains sober till everything is clear.

Will the two sons realize her deception?

Will she succeed to seduce the entire family?

DECEPTION

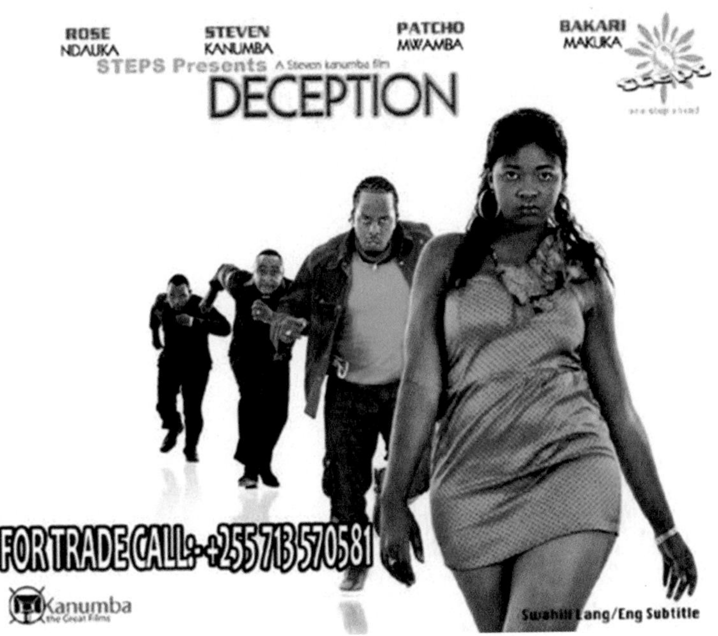

Deception: A movie that focus on the power of Lies. If you want to succeed, you must learn to love the truth. Otherwise, you will always leave open a door of deception for the enemy to take what is meant to be yours. What is the end of a deceitful life?

Devil Kingdom

Devil Kingdom: A movie that was acted and casted in the year 2011and left the viewers amazed with the plot. He worked with one of the leading Nollywood artist like Ramsey Nuoah.

A movie acted with a lot of brevity. The power of darkness verses the power of light. This depicts the consequences of serving Satan.

Avoid wicked and evil people. Don't open the door to the devil. Surround yourself with positive people.

What is the end of a man who worships the devil?

Is the devil real?

Will a man sell his soul to the devil in exchange of fame and money?

The Shock

The Shock: A lady is involved in a long distance relationship because her man is always traveling on business. After a long-wait for her relationship, she however gets tired and begins another relationship. One day she travels on a business trip to South Africa.

She soon discovers that her new lover also betrays her with other women once she travels. She decides to go back to her first relationship but she also finds out she is expecting. The unfaithful lover is eventually left with no one to love.

What is the test of a marriage?

Will you forgive a partner who has cheated you with another man?

Will you watch another man bring up your child because the woman you cheated on has rejected you?

A must watch movie for every movie fan.

Moses

Moses: Moses hates all women. His hatred has nothing to do with any woman, but due to his background. His parents did things that made him hate all women. He soon becomes a philosopher who only believes in science and not God.

Will you hate all the women just because of one woman who messed you up?

Big Dad

Big Dad: This features the importance of mothers in bringing up children.

Mothers have their own special role to play as well as father. A child needs both parents to grow up well.

Will a father alone give his children too love without their mother?

Because of you

Because of you: A movie that features the love of a husband to his wife and their day to day relationship.

The man is determined by all means to give his wife the best love in the world. He works, lives and only thinks of his wife.

Love is remarkable and knows everything about the loved person..

Love is ready to defend and protect in every way. Love that every human being will fight to have. A special movie that leaves every viewer stirred up and ready to do everything to have the same love.

NDOA YANGU

Ndoa yangu: A movie that features a marriage torn apart due to misfortunes. Lack of communication and unfaithfulness leads to tearing apart the love once shared.

Will a marriage counselor save this marriage?

Love and Power

Love and Power :A special movie that stirred up the viewers. Many said that Steven Kanumba predicted his own death in this film. The cast and the plot exactly replicated itself during his death.

Is it true that he predicted his death?

Watch this movie and compare with turn of events that surrounded his death and all the people who were involved.

Was his death a coincidence or pre-planned?

Steven Kanumba Was Set To Storm Hollywood

Other Trailers that never were;

The bleeding Sunshine; this was a trailer that Steven Kanumba was expected to be part of the crew. This trailer was expected to be filmed in several countries among them Ghana, Dubai and Egypt.

In this film, Steven was expected to feature together with other celebrated Hollywood actors.

The trailer had been written by Yaa Boaa Aning. The general manager of the movie was Prince Richard from Ghana.

Everyone anticipated seeing the first Tanzanian to feature in such a trailer. Prince Richard who by then was a U.S citizen had earlier met Steven Kanumba in a Zanzibar Festival. He got to experience his talents as Bongo movies featured in the same festival.

As a manager, he knew Steven had an incomparable talent.

This trailer was to later be premiered on big screens in several countries across the world.

In the same trailer, two other Tanzanian actors were expected to feature. Rose Ndauka and Lucy Komba had been chosen as they had displayed their talent too.

Apart from bleeding Sunshine, they were expected to feature in another trailer, Presidan First Love.

This trailer was about a great African leader who had shown prowess in his leadership. Steven Kanumba had been chosen to play as the head of security for this great African leader.

Another trailer was Challete. He was to feature together with Lucy Komba. This trailer was supposed to take his works as film personality to higher levels too.

In the movie industry, a lot as taking shaping as Bongo movies were to be included in major festival in the Unites States of America.

The auditions were already in progress and everything had taken shape to be birthed out. In Accra, Ghana, the team waited patiently to conduct the auditions for all members.

Steven Kanumba passed on exactly 10 hours before the long awaited audition. Everyone tried to reach him on his mobile phone, but all their efforts were futile.. That was a sad moment for the entire crew and all the actors who had known him personally. The future had just begun for him.

Death can only be likened to an enemy who will walk in when least expected. Steven Kanumba's dairy was already full but never to wake up to the tasks.

Bleeding Sunshine, Presidan First Love and Challete were enough tasks to take him away from Tanzania for more than six months. Ghana was not his destination, but he was expected to travel to several other countries. The entire team had their hopes shattered as they had lost an icon. No one had the capability to take his place.

Tanzania had not only lost a real son but the world was left empty with no one to fill the gap. Steven Kanumba had opted to unite the film industry by collaborating with actors from other countries.

He dreamt to initiate the first Ghanaian-East African film and also to feature in Hollywood movies. This had already taken shape as he had acted several movies with actors from other countries. Africa was already a home away from home as all actors were already working together.

Every arrangement and planning had been laid down before his death. This caused changed of plan.

No one had ever imagined that an icon of his caliber would die so soon.

This was not the end of the trailers, work had to go on.

The manager had to go an extra mile to get his replacement. Steven had displayed a unique talent that was of interest to all viewers.

Richard had not only drawn his interest on Steven Kanumba but also to many other actors in Bongo movies.

He had noticed a unique talent that was nowhere to be found. Mr. Richard had taken his initiative to fund all the trailers as he wanted to show the world this special talent he had seen. He also wanted to gather together a core of serious-minded actors and actresses, who were ready for the international stage.

He however wanted actors who could speak good English, as this was a language that was well articulated on the international stage.

This made other actors come on board too. These included Kenneth Ambani by the cast name Baraza from Kenya. Kenneth had gained his fame in early 90's for featuring in a Kenyan local drama popularly known as "Tausi". He was not only an actor but a personal friend of Steven Kanumba.

Others were Jessica Brown, Rose Ndauka, Lucy Komba, Mtunis, Ndubagwe "Thea" Misayo, Jacky Kisaka, Hashim Kambi, Emma Myamba and others.

About Bleeding Sunshine: A Hollywood Thriller on Human Trafficking and Child slavery

This is about how millions of innocent people are dragged into slavery and later end up being sold away.

This focuses on how information is shared about the victims and their eventuality.

Features a young girl who is adapted from her poor family to a dangerous sophisticated world of human trafficking.

Yaa Boaa Aning, the scriptwriter had written the film's script while doing a **research**. While doing the research, she came across an article that inspired her to investigate more on human trafficking.

At the same time, she loved the beautiful locations in Ghana that were very good for movie shooting.

The movie was to involve actors of different nationalities as it was expected to sell internationally.

The film's African cast included **Hotel** Rwanda star Hakeem Kae-Kazim, "2011(AMAA), Best Actress - Ama K."2011 Pan African best Actor- Chris Attoh, 2010 (AMAA), Best Actor–Adjetey Anang (Pusher), 1996 Oakland Black Film Achievement Winner - Amonobea Dodoo, 2011 Tanzania"s Best Actor -**Steven Kanumba**, 1998 USIS Award Winner-Omar Sheriff Captan, Amonobea Dodoo–1996 OakLand Black Film Achievement Winner with new-comer Suzzy Norbile,, Jasmine Baroudi, Lady Arafua, Afro-Soul sensation Katou whose single" Happy Endings" had just set the R&B charts on fire & Lucy Kwao with other African casts.

Adjetey Anang played the character of Captain Addo, a fisherman, the father of Suzzy, the girl who was trafficked overseas.

Yaa Boaa had her **career** in advertising in New York which gave her no creativity expression; she then decided to try her luck at fashion show production with some of the most famous houses in the world–Giorgio Armani, BCBG and Betsey Johnson and others.

Fashion styling production opened doors for her to film costuming, which ultimately exposed her to the film industry. She started working with popular working with directors such as Michael Mann, Bill Condon and John Singleton. She finally became a script writer due to her interactions.

She also became a director. In 2009 she wrote and directed award winning movie, The Prince of Venice. After this, she did several others.

She is famous on Hollywood movies and Television series. Steven Kanumba was walking on same footsteps that Yaa Boaa had already trailed. He had shown the zeal and determination to do even better. Her fashion career had equipped her too with costume knowledge.

Working together with Richard who had already known Steven Kanumba was even of a higher advantage.

Steven Kanumba also got the opportunity to audition for Big Brother 4. A chance that only selected and few lucky artists get to have once in a life time.

Steven Charles Kanumba as director 1

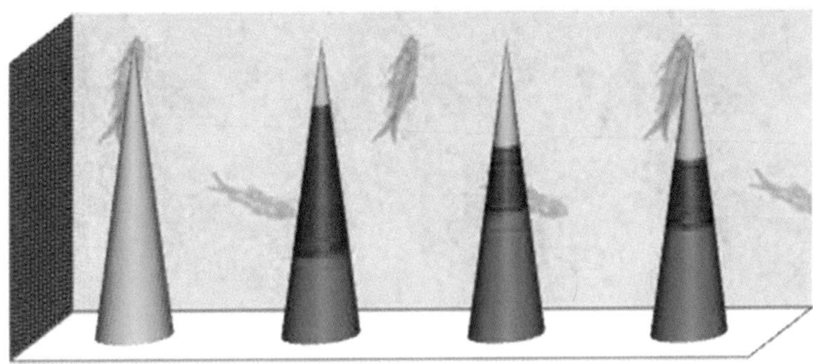

Steve Charles Kanumba as Director 2

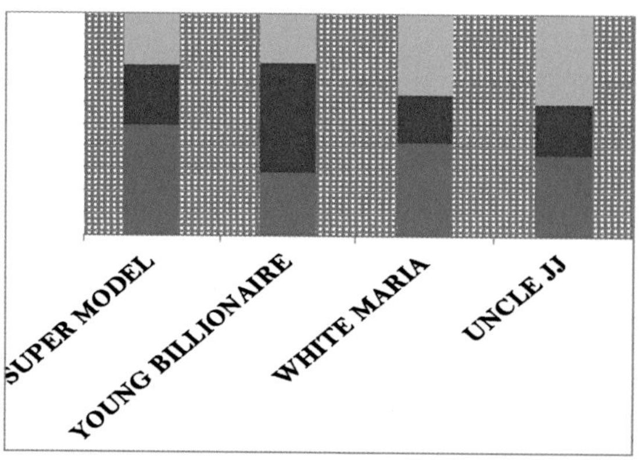

AS DIRECTOR AGAIN 3

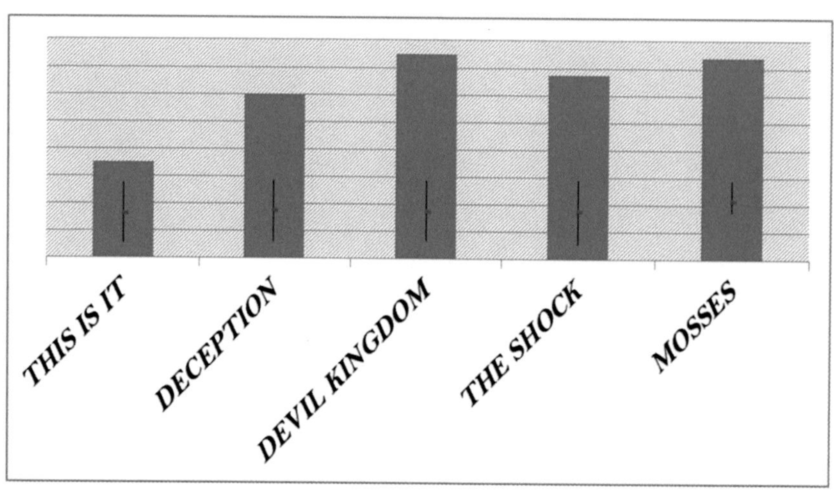

Steven Charles Kanumba as Writer

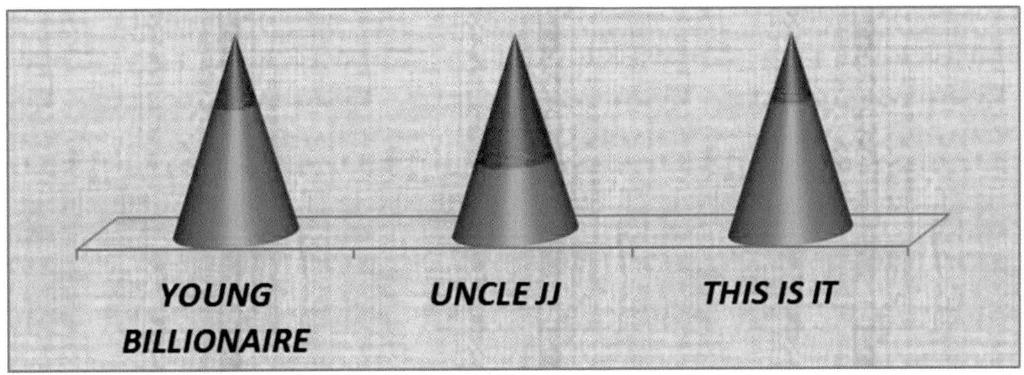

Steven Charles Kanumba Awards

Among awards won by artiste Kanumba are IJUMAA Sexiest male bachelor of the year-2006, Best Actor of the Year (Baab Kubwa Magazine)-2006 The Best Actor in Tanzania (Hollywood John Wayne International Awards)-2007, Honorary Award (Tanzania Film Vinara Awards)-2008, Best Actor-2007-2008 (SHIVIWATA) and best actor and best director -Film Central-2010.

He received an honorary award for the great achievement he had made to his country as well.

The picture shows Thea and Kanumba happy after receiving their awards outside Jubilee hall.

FC AWARDS 2010

FC Awards 2010; this was what he had to say on that day.

"Keep your dream alive. Understand that to achieve anything requires faith and belief in oneself. Remember that all things are possible for those who believe. I don't believe in luck. I have never banked on it and I'm afraid of people who do. Luck to me is something else. Hard work and realizing what an opportunity is and what not an opportunity is."

The fruit of hard work

"The success you want is yours, only if you have the courage, the drive, the determination to put in the hard work you need to succeed! If you work just for money, you'll never make it, but if you love what you're doing and always put the customer first, success will be yours".

The fruits of success always grow on the tree of hard work.

People don't succeed because their lucky. They succeed because they set goals and work toward those goals. They plan for success.

The great Steven Kanumba also said, "Sometimes you will never know the value of a moment, until it becomes a memory. Sometimes it could also be too late to tell a person about that too."

STEVEN CHARLES KANUMBA'S RED CARPET MOMENTS

These were his words, "Even if we have the ability to move mountains, if we don't love one another in Tanzania, then it is nothing of importance. What is in the heart is what manifests outside every human being. This must be shown by our love and actions towards each other. This film industry is a gift that God has given us. One day we shall be accountable for this same gift. God has the ability to take it away from us if we do not utilize it well. Read the book of Corinthians from the Holy Bible and see how God is generous in distributing these gifts to His children".

Kanumba was a diligent man in his work.

He received an honorary award for the great achievement he had made to his country as well.

STEVEN KANUMBA AND OTHER PROJECTS IN THE COMMUNITY

Steven Kanumba was also named as the **Oxfam GROW Ambassador** on 2nd of June 2011.

Oxfam is a British charity founded in 1942, dedicated to helping victims of famine and natural disasters as well as raising living standards in developing countries.

It is also an international confederation of 17 organizations working in approximately 94 countries worldwide to find solutions to poverty and what it considers as injustice around the world. In all Oxfam's actions the ultimate goal is to enable people to exercise their rights and manage their own lives.

It works directly with communities and seeks to influence the powerful, to ensure that poor people can improve their lives and livelihoods and have a say in decisions that affect them. Each organization works together internationally to achieve a greater impact through collective efforts.

Steven Charles Kanumba in one of his duties as an Oxfam GROW ambassador.

Star Times Ambassador in Tanzania.

On October 2nd, 2011 He was endorsed as Star Times Ambassador in Tanzania.

Steven Kanumba id s awarded a blackberry phone by Zantel for having being a good ambassador of their company in Tanzania.

STEVEN KANUMBA'S DEATH

A fateful Friday, that was supposed to be a celebrated Friday between two lovers, ended up being a disaster. Steven Kanumba with his girlfriend Elizabeth Michael, Lulu, prepared themselves to go and enjoy themselves in a club. In the middle of the night, the girlfriend got calls that she decided to answer. Furious about the call, a fight between the two lovers ensued. This was not a normal fight as it was fatal. What ensued was death. He fell in the midst of the argument in compromising situations and was rushed to the hospital in an unconscious state. He died of brain injury the following Saturday morning. One of the doctors at the Muhimbili National Hospital (MNH) who participated in the autopsy said due to brain injury, the film icon died on the spot.

Other sources said a witness was in Steven Kanumba's house when Lulu attempted to get outside his bedroom but was refrained by him by pulling her back. Lulu informed the witness that the great Steven Charles Kanumba had fallen and he proceeded to his room and found him lying down. He called his private doctor who after examining him said he was already dead.

Lulu was arraigned in court on the following Wednesday after his death. Speaking to 'Daily News' Zakayo Magulu who doubled as a film Editor and Assistant Director said the last scene of the film where Kanumba dies, is exactly the way he died in real life, which was previously not in the original script. The last scene of the original script of the film 'Power and Love' was to have him seen walking along a lonely road feeling sad, after a dispute with the woman he loved in the film. Kanumba had said, that the ending was not mesmerizing, thereby proposing a scene where he would be pushed by the woman he loved and died in the process.

Mr. Magulu explained all these in details as he was present when Steven Kanumba argued about this. Expounding on the 'Power and Love' film, Mr. Magulu said Kanumba had donated his kidney to a woman, 'Irene Paul' whom they had fallen in love. Later on in the film, the woman, Irene Paul, goes back to her previous boyfriend; a dispute ensued prompting the woman to push Kanumba and he dropped dead. Mr. Magulu said the same friend who went to see Kanumba when he died in the film whom he identified as Kupa, was also there when Kanumba was being taken to the mortuary in real life. The same doctor, whom Mr. Magulu identified by one name, Pancras who was also in the film to examine Kanumba when he was pushed by the woman he loved and died, was the same doctor who was called to examine the late icon, when he was pushed by his girlfriend, fell down and died in real life. "Everything happened just like it was in the last scene of the Power and Love film," he explained.

His final journey will enter the annals of Tanzanian history as one of the most attended funerals in their time. A Hollywood source revealed intriguing details of contracts that was set to make him one of the greatest stars in that region.

According to documents obtained exclusively by the Beat, the deal had been sealed at 5pm on Friday and Steven Charles Kanumba was on his way to becoming one of the biggest cash spinners in East and Central Africa, in the film industry.

20,000 people attended his funeral; some other sources estimated the total to be 30,000 people. He was described as Tanzania's most popular film star and the funeral was believed to be the biggest since that of the country's founding father Julius Nyerere in October 18th 1999.

He did not require a bunch of degrees or PHDs in order to be famous but rather it was the commitment and dedication to his work in the movie industry that made him excel at such a young age. His death was just unbelievable.

Dar residents and mourners queue to pay their last respect to the great local film star Steven Charles Kanumba at his funeral.

That day, he realized a lot of sales for his own acted movies.

Government dignitaries who attended the funeral included President Jakaya Kikwete who praised the deceased for having made a big impact in a very short time in the Tanzanian movie industry. He said the great Steven Charles Kanumba played a great role in developing the movie industry and marketing Tanzania abroad through motion pictures.

His movies offered great lessons and were loved not only by the elderly but also the youngsters due to their content

Vincent Kigosi a good friend to the great Steven Charles Kanumba well known by the name "Ray" was heard on EATV saying that together with the great Steven Charles Kanumba, they used to stage the Kaole Sanaa group the hard way while carrying their clothes in plastic bags on their way to shooting the films

He added that they had vigor and zeal to achieve something in life and that he left tearless eyes to most of his fans and the country at large

At his tender age, he managed to bring the movie industry in Tanzania and tune Tanzanians minds into watching locally produced movies rather than the Hollywood and Nollywood movies that hitherto dominated the Tanzanian market.

President Jakaya Kikwete delays trip

During a condolence visit at the actor's house at Sinza Vatican in Dar es Salaam, President **Kikwete** had this to say about the actor

"I have come to join you in mourning the great Steven Charles Kanumba whom we have known each other during his movie star career. I invited him in a luncheon in Dodoma together with some of his friends who have been cooperating in their movie starring career. We are bound to miss the great Steven Charles Kanumba who has left the world at a very young age, but I believe this is the will of God. Please try to come to terms with this hard time. May his soul rest in perfect peace Amen."

This was also a very sad moment for Nollywood. Several of them fainted at his funeral.

It was a very hard moment during his funeral for everyone.

Dar residents and mourners queue to pay their last respect to the great local film star Steven Charles Kanumba at his funeral.

Some of the most affected were Irene Uwoya who lost consciousness and had to be carried away.

Since, Elizabeth Michael, lulu by her cast name, was the last person to be with Steven Kanumba had to be taken to court.

She denied to have caused his death but charged with manslaughter charges as she had urgued that thay quarreled just as any other couple.

She was charged with unintentional killing of Kanumba on April 7, 2012 at his home in Kinondoni District, Dar es Salaam. This was a sad moment for Steven Kanumba's family as all they wanted was justice for their son.

Her lawyer was up to let the world know that she had a relationship with the late Steven Kanumba.

This was later confirmed from many other sources and it was concluded that she had been welcomed to visit the house of the deceased on the fateful day.

This was not only a case of two families, but the whole world was keen to know the truth.

Her pictures were everywhere on the internet for the conviction of murder. Her case had heavy charges as it revolved around murder. She was remanded for seven months in prison and her case was eventually heard at the High Court. She was released on bail after securing two Government employees as her sureties.

Each of two sureties signed a bond of 20 million Tanzanian Shillings.

Elizabeth Michael (Lulu), The Last person to see and interact closely with the Great Steven Charles Kanumba.

The name Lulu is one popular topic in Tanzania both in media and real social life, since the death of The Great actor, Steven Kanumba. At a tender age, she found herself in a fix that no one would believe her word.

DIRECTING A MOVIE

The following are very important key points on directing movies.

Actors and actresses need to be reminded several times on their roles in the play. In most cases the motive may not match with the dialogue.

This is called **subtext**. When a character says that they hate the other person, it may not necessarily mean that they hate them. They may actually mean they love them very much. The director has a great role in making sure that he directs such areas skillfully.

Subtext is not a difficult concept: It represents what the character means rather that what he or she says.

Competitive actors and actresses may not be a solution for a successful cast. Working with the most talented of them can also be a good idea.

However, it does not mean that they are the best to use in a play. Some may be very difficult to direct. A good actor or actress must always love to be directed.

Another important point to consider is how to talk to actors and actresses when directing them.

It is impolite to shout on them, talk rudely to them or even discriminate them when directing. Politeness and good language is very important.

Most of them are very sensitive to publicly said comments. A good director must always remain professional. He must not be hot tempered or easily angered but very composed. That attracts every actor and actress in working with such a director. That is real mentorship.

Directing actors and actresses

This industry requires a lot **of self sacrifice and determination.** A profound choice of both actors and actresses is required: Very popular and talented actors and actresses are a very important choice.

They carry the day even when they have nothing to say. They catch the eye of the viewer. No one would want to miss the opportunity to just see a celebrity in the film industry.

Popular and talented actors and actresses have common characteristics. They have a strong personality; they attract the audience without even saying anything. They are not overnight heroes.

Majority have worked their way to the top. Others are naturally talented. Choosing less expensive actors and actresses is a very wise decision. They are easy to nurture. Once a director gets this kind of actors and actresses, he or she must learn to work with them progressively.

A very important factor: No actor or actress can be replaced by another; each of them is unique in his or her own way. Professional actors and actresses are always different from the rest. It is always good to note cheap will always be very expensive in the end.

A good actor and actress know that he or she cannot make it alone. A director must not be torn apart by what he or she wants and what the actor or actress wants. This can be dangerous. Professionalism requires confidence in directing and being directed. Most successful actors and actresses know their work is to be directed and not what they think they should do. They complain less and work tirelessly with their directors. That is a spirit of a teacher student relationship. This makes each play their part effectively.

Directing a play is as important as casting a play. That is why it is important to get focused actors and actresses who know what they want out of their career. There is no room for compromise as the world expects to watch nothing but the best.

That is why one cannot avoid working with the best of the best. This makes the director in raising his standards too. It also becomes less tedious in directing them as they learn fast. This gives each of them a room for excellence too.

For every amazing performance there is also an outstanding output. Focused actors and actresses spend time memorizing their parts well and struggle less on stage. Creativity and originality is what makes the difference.

A good actor and actress will not necessarily cram sentence by sentence but will try to paraphrase it to make the sentence better. This makes the performance more real than just a play.

It is always good to work on the strengths of the actors and actresses rather than their weaknesses. A good working atmosphere is also very important and the director must always maintain it. Every person involved must be praised. The camera operators, dolly grips, crane operators and all the rest are very important for a play to be complete. Let praise be done publicly so that one is encouraged.

Directions and corrections must be done privately and politely. Every professional is a human being and must be accorded their respect. This creates confidence in every member of the crew. It also gives the director an opportunity to be trusted as a mentor. Best results will always be found when such a relationship co- exists.

Movie acting is a career. Film industry is not only an art but also a career like being a teacher or a pilot. This means that it can be a full time job for a professional. A professional will give out their best as they know that is their life. An actor or actress who is not committed is not the best to work with. They will always give the wrong results. A director must be careful, not to become very close friends with the actors and actresses.

This increases level of respect and professionalism. If it happens there will always be a conflict of ideas. Most actors and actresses will try to get the attention of the director to get some major roles on the basis of friendship. This must never happen.

A good director will go an extra mile and get the right talent without any favors. This also tames a good actor and actress to expect less from any project.

This also makes a director adhere strictly in bringing out the talent expected. This does not leave out the young and less talented actors and actresses. They also need to be nurtured to bring out their best.

Every actor and actress has a hidden talent that needs to be discovered. A good director will do everything to discover it and bring it out to the world.

Editing movies.

This is a skill that every movie director must have. This calls for him or her to be a professional planner. He or she must go to class and learn all skills involved in editing a movie.

A real director is not only concerned with the members of the cast but the final audience. Cutting actions must be professional and coherent. All shots must smoothly follow one another without making the viewer feel disgusted.

The Screenplay

The characters:

A director must consider texture as an important aspect. Any play must not just be a play. The audience must flow with the play as though it was a real life situation. This makes the audience remain attentive and ready to follow any other episodes bearing the same characters. The movie industry must sound and appear as real to all the viewers. Most of the audience draws lessons and habits from the story lines. That is why the best performance must always be upheld.

Triple repeats

A triple repeats is a term to refer to words used three times in a screen play. This brings clear and better understanding to the audience.

It also makes the audience to connect and know the characters very well. Human brain works like a computer. It will only remember what has been repeated and not what was said once.

Plot symmetry

This where part of the film is repeated later within the same film after showing up at the beginning of a play.

For example, at the beginning of a play, the protagonist is seen performing an action with other characters. This gives the audience an expectant curiosity to know what happens. Every audience needs to get a taste of the play in order to get the desire to follow up the whole movie.

Why is plot symmetry so satisfying for the audience?

Same reason as for triple repeats and dialogue symmetry: by giving the brain a generous dose of carefully designed narrative pattern, a feeling of intense understanding is induced, and as humans we can't get enough of that. The brain must be constantly get puffed with curiousity.

Triple repeats, dialogue symmetry and plot symmetry are very important and must be carefully considered in any play.

Preparations made by Movie Directors

A director must understand the scene before having the directorial vision and planning shots.

A scene must be accompanied with good shots and cuts. A good scene is what differentiates the sharks and the dwarfs. A good scene will not only be eye catching, but also good for camera work and editing. This might be expensive too but it is worth investing into it.

A good director always thinks of where to do the shooting while directing a scene. That calls for creativity too in every director's visual mind. The choice of a venue for shooting is determined on early stages of directing a play.

The director must get a clear mental picture of the venues as he or she directs the play.

Therefore, shooting and editing a movie go hand in hand.

In every script, every scene is unique in its own way.

A well developed script has several scenes. Every scene serves the purpose of developing characters, advancing the plot of the play; make an important point about the play or the three of them at once.

Both the director and the actors and actresses must understand perfectly what is required of each scene.

The Pre-Production Checklist: The following are points to consider in order making most of the shoot.

Start by writing a shot list of all the requirements needed.

This is a numbered list of shots that includes a description of the shot in terms of composition, camera movement and other issues. Any other instructions on directions for actors and actresses can be on the same shot list. The shot list may vary from one director to another.

Directions for actors and actresses

A director must develop clear concepts on the various roles and types of performances expected from each actor or actress. This must be a very detailed description for every actor or actress.

The Production design

Every director must work hand in hand with a production designer. This includes usage of painting, art magazines, quality photographs and other films as well.

A production designer must also be provided with form of photography in order to bring out the best.

Location scouting

Depending on the type of project and scenes, one must travel to several locations to bench mark the best location for a shoot. Other plays may cost a lot of travelling depending on the number of scenes.

Finding locations is a difficult task in itself, because one needs to find the right location at the right price for every scene in a project. This can take a long time before the final decision is made.

Pre-visualization videos

This involves shooting for the purpose of testing.

This is done with low quality equipments and it involves a minimal expenditure or no cost at all.

This can be done locally, and even a director can be assisted by relatives.

Sound recording tips:

Good quality sound is also an important aspect.

One of the biggest shortcomings of many videos is quality sound. The technique and the location of sound production determine the quality of sound. Production of quality sound based on location is a wide topic.

Choose the right type of microphone

Recording high quality location sound one requires the right type of microphone: ultra-directional for external locations, directional (shorter) for interiors, and non-directional for cramped interiors.

It has been observed that, the more directional the microphone, the greater the extent to which it selectively picks up sounds from its front end, and the higher the signal-to-noise ratio will be; but it is worth noting that excessively directional microphones will pick up too much echo in right interior locations, so the right compromise must be struck in such situations. The Audio- Technica BP4073 Lightweight Shotgun Microphone is a very good dialogue microphone – Most professionals like to use it.

Audio- Technica BP4073 Lightweight Shotgun Microphone

It has specifically been designed for use in broadcasting, film/TV production and theater sound reinforcement applications Direct-coupled, balanced output ensures a clean signal even in high-output conditions Innovative acoustic design provides same directivity as microphones up to 50% longer Switchable 80 Hz hi-pass filter & 10 dB pad Rugged housing made of lightweight structural-grade aluminum alloy compliant free from all substances specified in the EU directive on the reduction of hazardous substances.

The microphone must be placed close to the actor's mouth all the time.

After choosing the right microphone, one must focus on producing clean and high quality location dialogue **by** placing the microphone as close as possible to the subject. This helps in avoiding any background noise that may interfere with the subject's voice. The microphone must be positioned in such a way that it is overhead, pointing downwards at the subject's mouth. The other best choice is to position the microphone just below the bottom frame edge, with the microphone pointing upwards at the actor's mouth.

It is good to shoot several takes of every setup.

One should do several takes of each scene, regardless of how well and perfect the actors and the actresses are performing, as this helps in good sound production of every scene involved. Sometimes this production can be in a noisy environment too, so this will help in choosing the best by the end of the day. This makes it easy to choose the best of the best. One must listen to the sound during and after each take on every location, though some of them might be very annoying to listen to. This will help in eliminating the unnecessary and choosing the best.

One must also record at least 30 seconds of ambient sound.

For every location and every shot in that location, one must record at least 30 seconds of ambient sound. That means there will be silent recording of about 30 minutes where everyone will be quiet. This is called **ambient**

sound, and the "silent recording" will be different for every location and every setup in that location (The loudness of ambient sound depends in part on how close the microphone is from the subject, which in turn depends on how the shot is also framed).

The onboard microphone should be out of the question as it is of poor quality.

This is the type of microphone mounted on cameras and it has the worst sound production. It is simple and easy to use but of very poor sound production.

The fact that it is mounted on the camera means that the microphone is placed far away from the subject. It attracts all echo hidden noises making it the last option a professional will want to use. The microphone must always be close to the subject's mouth.

Sometimes the onboard microphone can be used for the entire shoot and later the poor location is replaced by a clean dialogue re-recorded in a studio. However this is very expensive and time consuming. The sharks in the film industry use location sound, only opting to automatic dialogue replacement when it's absolutely necessary. A well-recorded location sound is the best thing to listen to.

The Movie Making Process

Development

This is the most tedious and most involving stage of any movie. This is where the foundations are laid and all elements are assembled for the whole project. This is the real movie making process and is written to be relevant to independent movie makers .This will vary from one system to another. For example, Hollywood-style will be different from Nollywood style.

Development may constitute of several processes too. This includes;

Story development / treatment / scriptment / plot points / structure

In this phase story of the movie is developed. Every scriptwriter has a personal way of developing a story. The structure and the plot of the story is however important. . He or she must be creative enough to develop a peculiar and an original script. He or she must avoid copying or following another scriptwriter's story line.

Having developed the basic structure of the story, for most scriptwriters the next step usually involves writing a scene-by-scene outline of the whole movie. Many writers use an index card for each scene, because they are easy to arrange and re-arrange on a board. This is a liberal stage and one can decide to use their own method of arrangement.

Writing the screenplay

Only the original writer has a clear vision of the structure, plot points and scene outline of his story line. Writing must not be a priority for any professional script writer. This can make one lose content or run dry after writing the first few pages.

There are also several soft wares that assist in writing and formatting the screenplay. They may be expensive but worth investing into them.

Re-writing the screenplay

Great scripts are not written, they are re-written. This may take time but eventually the final draft will be the best. Most professional writers will even write more than five times before they get the final copy. Patience and creativity are key factors in getting the best.

Financing the movie

Nothing comes from free. Money is the principal thing for success in any industry. One must have enough capital to finance all the activities involved. This can be done on an individual level or sometimes it can be outsourced from sponsors.

On rare occasions will movie makers fund their own movie. When a movie is well developed, it will definitely have a good film distribution channel hence make good profits. Every movie maker must have a good marketer in order good fruits of their hardwork.

Pre-production

This process must only begin when the money for financing every step is available. This will minimize lapses and bad bills.

This is accompanied by carefully selecting the right and key crew members. The movie maker must be well talented to avoid him or her getting mixed up. Pre-production may also have several activities. These include;

Casting

This involves choosing the right characters for the right roles. Specifications of actor's ability are a key consideration. The ability to exhibit the right talent must carry the day. Friendship, as mentioned earlier must not be a factor to consider in this level. The search for a talent might even involve undertaking auditions to select the best. The level of experience of an actor or actress on stage may also be a factor to consider whenchoosing the casting crew.

Choosing Locations

The locations must be selected carefully. Good locations come with a hefty budget as good places must be paid for. This has also become easier with time as there are also film location agents who help in choosing the right location at a fee without so many struggles. There are also disadvantages involved in choosing the right venues through film location agents. Their taste might not be the movie maker's taste.

Their fee might also be too high. They have extensive libraries of location to suite generally any movie.

Shot list

This includes list of shots, local length time, camera movement, and other important aspects Storyboards may also be included. They bear and communicate the vision of the movie to the target group. The shot list will always vary from one professional to another.

Location scouting

This is the most enjoyable part of movie production. It is sometimes known as "Tech Scout" This involves just visiting as many locations as possible then comparing all of them to choose the best. This helps the movie maker to have a wider variety of choices. This also helps the movie maker to interact with the owners of the selected locations and get the legal permission to use the location in case it suits the need. The movie maker may also choose to be accompanied by the members of the crew to help in exchanging ideas. This will help in minimizing any mistakes that can be corrected if done as a team. The crew members must also go through a small training on own to conduct themselves as they visit different locations. In some areas an introductory letter from relevant authorities may be required.

Scheduling

Good planning leads to success. In most cases a professional planner is hired to do the scheduling of events.

Production design

This involves the arrangement done on the chosen locations, purchasing anything needed to add value to the production process and general preparedness. The costume designers also appear in this stage.

Production

This is the principle process. It involves a lot of photography and shooting works. This may be enjoyable stage depending on the motivation of the crew members.

Setting Up the Principal photography

Time must be observed by the crew members as locations may be on appointments. Minimal supervision is needed on this level as each crew member must be responsible on their parts.

Rehearsal

This is giving a taste of the real thing. It must be done with a lot of keenness. This stage is taken with a lot of weight as it must be reviewed thoroughly for approval. This is when real shots really take shape to reality.

Setting up shots

This involves majorly the camera crew being directed on camera movements and any details involving the camera. Good and quality cameras are required for quality work.

Checking the shot/takes

After every shot, the director reviews the shots/takes on the video monitor and decides what needs to be used or dismissed. The process is repeated until the director is satisfied with the best of the best.

This may also be reviewed in an editing room. This helps in getting and capturing a clear picture of what is required. At this level any director must be have learnt great lessons that need to be an upper hand for any future projects.

Editing

Movie editing is a skill. This will involve different types of soft wares depending on the level of investment. The film language must clearly be taken seriously and any other language translations need to be undertaken in a professional manner.

Sound mixing

Sound mixing involves adding any necessary sound effects, setting the level of each soundtrack and making the soundtrack as seamless as possible. This adds flavor to the movie and creates attention to the viewer.

Music

The composition and production of the movie's music is another aspect that we always enjoy. This will depend on the theme of the movie. Talented composers and singers who are versed with the play are the best to work with.

The pace of the music, the type of musical instruments, the mood of the music and the starting and stopping aspects must be well outlined. Music composers bring out the feelings and help the viewer flow with the movie. A good director will bench mark and listen to different sound tracks and choose the best. Listen to the demo tracks and suggest changes. The music composer must also be directed to get the best.

Test screenings

Once the project is done, testing it with close workmates is highly recommended. This involves watching and analyzing before the release. This gives the director extra confidence of his work.

Movie distribution

Honest distributers and marketers are needed to start the sale. Advertisements and posters can be of great help to let the world know of the new product in the market. Piracy of the completed work must be on watch list. Every country has laws that govern offenders of film industry. The marketers and distributers must be also on the lookout for the original works and the screen recorded works. These are generally sold on the streets at a throw away price. Film festivals also promote sales. A certain amount is charged as entry fee to watch on big screens in the cinema halls. They too generate great financial returns.

APPRECIATION PAGE

The compilation of this great piece of work was not a simple task. First and foremost, I want to give **glory to God**, the maker of the universe, who gave me the opportunity to be able to give to the world this gift.

Flora Mutegoa, the mother of Steven Kanumba, a great woman who was bold to raise her son and even after his death, she is proud to tell to the world that all things are possible before God. She has embraced the fact that the same God who gave her the same great son, he is able to give her strength to face the world. Steven Kanumba's two elder sisters **Vedastina Mshumbusi** and **Abela Kajumulo**. Not to forget the great love and support from **Otmar Peter** and **Issaya Kandonga**.

Kaole Sanaa group who gave Kanumba the opportunity to explore his great talent, which eventually brought smiles on many.

Mtitu Game for tirelessly working with the Late to produce his great acted movies.

His co- actors. The list is endless. Without them, he could not shine alone. **Roy Vincent Kigosi, Wema sepetu, Jb Stephan Jacob, Steve Nyerere, Single mtambarike, Rose Ndauka, Lucy Komba, Ivon Cheryl Monalisa, Aunt Ezekiel, Iren Uwoya, Jackline Holper, Elizabethe Michael Lulu, Patcho Mwamba** and others in Bongo Movies.

Across the International scene, **Kenneth Ambani** from Kenya who was his great friend and attended several auditions with him. **Cassie Kabwita** from Zambia, who was mentored by Steven Kanumba but never met him face to face.

Prince Richard, Nigeria Mercy Johnson, Nkiru Silvanus, Femi Ogedegbe and Ramsey Nuah from Nigeria.

The Government of Tanzania that gave full support to their son. The **president, Jakaya Mrisho Kikwete**, His wife the first lady of tanzania, **Salma Kikwete**, The Vice President, **Dr. Mohamed Gharib Bilal**, and the minister for culture and sport, **Emmanuel Nchimbi** among others.

Special thanks to **Oxfarm, Zantel, Startimes** and **John Wyne** for being there every time in bringing up the star to be what he was. Great companies that have shown they are here to serve humanity.

About author

Story writer: by Emmanuel E Zirimwabagabo from Canada.

Emmanuel is the author of book what goes around comes around. He is a written many other books that are yet to be published

Emmanuel E Zirimwabagabo was born in Uvira, Congo DRC, the civil war that tore apart the Democratic Republic of Congo, separated him from his family for over 6 years. Emmanuel is presently employed in Northern Alberta, Canada in the Oil Sands Industry. He has made his home, with his family, in Edmonton, Alberta, Canada.

After arriving in Edmonton in 2009 his proficiency in French made it possible for him to continue his education and complete his high school at Maurice Lavalle. When attending school he was one the few students picked to attend a program in Ottawa, Ontario from the Forum for Young Canadians to study the processes of theGovernment of Canada. Emmanuel was also one of two students picked to attend the Explore Program International Education in Vancouver, British Columbian.

Along with Emmanuel's life experiences in Congo and his immigration to Canada he has many more from his travels to Tanzania, Burundi, Uganda, Rwanda and Qatar.

Would you like to preserve your life or that of a loved one or other honored person in a book? Your life is unique and deserves to be preserved forever. Episcopere Emmanuel provides professional book writing services to individuals and corporations to write personal histories, biographies and memoirs.

To preserve your own history in your memoir that of a loved one or of someone you admire in a book is the ultimate tribute to a life well lived and the best gift you can possibly give. We professionally write your memoir, biography or autobiography.

If you fail to pass on what you've accomplished or learned, what will be your legacy? As your loved ones age important memories will fade and eventually be lost forever. Don't let this happen.

Although we write celebrity biographies and memoirs, you don't need to be famous to preserve your life in a book. A life well lived is worthy of preservation in a printed book. Let us write your biography or memoir.

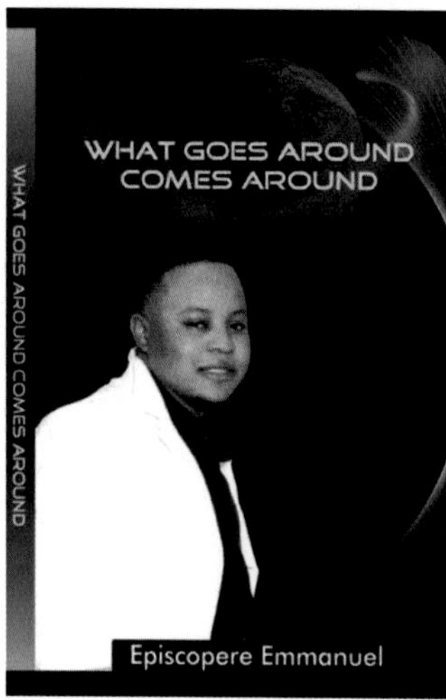

Feel free to contact Author Emmanuel, He speak English, French and Swahili.
Contact phone number: +1780 718 0989
www.authoremmanuelz.com
Email: lubalaemmanuel8@gmail.com
Book translated and edited by Eden Translators International, Mombasa Kenya

EDEN TRANSLATORS INTERNATIONAL is a language services agency which provides high quality language services in African, European and Asian languages. We translate books and documents from any language to the desired language on the face of planet earth.

It is based in Mombasa, Kenya but its linguists are found everywhere in the world. EDEN TRANSLATORS INTERNATIONAL rates are reasonably affordable. Each of its language experts has a university degree in translation and linguistics, and others a masters degree too, making the services we offer of the highest quality.

Name: Linah Wakungi from Kenya
Contact: + 254 726 838 822 or +254 414 479 989
Email: info@edentranslators.com
Website: www.edentranslators.com
Linah Wakungi from Kenya

Printed in the United States
By Bookmasters